Next Generation
ENERGY

LIVING IN A SUSTAINABLE WAY

Green Communities

Megan Kopp

CRABTREE
Publishing Company
www.crabtreebooks.com

W9-CMN-114

Crabtree Publishing Company

www.crabtreebooks.com

Author: Megan Kopp

Editors: Sarah Eason, Jen Sanderson,
and Shirley Duke

Proofreader: Katie Dicker and Wendy Scavuzzo

Editorial director: Kathy Middleton

Design: Paul Myerscough and Geoff Ward

Cover design: Paul Myerscough

Photo research: Sarah Eason and Jen Sanderson

Prepress technician: Margaret Amy Salter

Print coordinator: Margaret Amy Salter

Consultant: Richard Spilsbury, degree in Zoology,
30 years as an author and editor of educational
science books

Written and produced for Crabtree Publishing
by Calcium Creative

Photo Credits:

t=Top, bl=Bottom Left, br=Bottom Right

Dreamstime: Achim Baqué: pp. 10–11; Americanspirit: pp. 6–7;
Angela Ravaioli: p. 12; Bidouze Stéphane: p. 11; Brett Critchley:
pp. 12–13, 28–29; Helenamiler86: pp. 22–23; Jeffrey Banke: pp.
3, 16–17; Luciano Mortula: p. 22; Lunamarina: p. 7; Monkey
Business Images: pp. 24–25; Paul Prescott: p. 24; Petarneychev: p.
26; Rrodrickbeiler p. 18; William87: pp. 1, 14–15, 30–31; Xxlphoto:
p. 6; Zalakdagli: pp. 4–5; Shutterstock: Andrea Izzotti: p. 10;
Andrei Shumskiy: p. 28; Anweber: p. 21; Dario Sabljak: p. 27;
Grimgram: p. 19; Gui Jun Peng: pp. 18–19; Howamo: pp. 20–21;
John Wollwerth: p. 4; Matty Symons p. 16; Mike Flippo pp. 26–27;
Monticello pp. 3, 17; Mopic: p. 8; Mostovyi Sergii Igorevich: p. 9;
Mypokcik: p. 14; PhotoStockImage: p. 25; Trekandshoot: pp. 8–9,
32; Umberto Shtanzman: p. 15; Violetkaipa: p. 13; Voyagerix: p. 20;
Wikimedia Commons: Studio804: p. 23.

Cover: Dreamstime: William87.

Library and Archives Canada Cataloguing in Publication

Kopp, Megan, author
    Living in a sustainable way : green communities /
Megan Kopp.

(Next generation energy)
Includes index.
Issued in print and electronic formats.
ISBN 978-0-7787-2000-3 (bound).--
ISBN 978-0-7787-2008-9 (paperback).--
ISBN 978-1-4271-1643-7 (pdf).--
ISBN 978-1-4271-1635-2 (html)

    1. Sustainable living--Juvenile literature. 2.
Environmental protection--Citizen participation--Juvenile
literature. I. Title.

GE195.5.K67 2015   j333.72   C2015-903226-1
                                      C2015-903227-X

Library of Congress Cataloging-in-Publication Data

Kopp, Megan.
 Living in a sustainable way : green communities / Megan Kopp.
    pages cm. -- (Next generation energy)
 Includes index.
 ISBN 978-0-7787-2000-3 (reinforced library binding : alk. paper) --
ISBN 978-0-7787-2008-9 (pbk. : alk. paper) --
ISBN 978-1-4271-1643-7 (electronic pdf : alk. paper) --
ISBN 978-1-4271-1635-2 (electronic html : alk. paper)
1. Environmentalism--Juvenile literature. 2. Energy conservation-
-Juvenile literature. 3. Sustainable living--Juvenile literature. 4.
Community life--Environmental aspects--Juvenile literature.
I. Title.

GE195.5.K673 2016
333.79--dc23

                                2015022000

Crabtree Publishing Company

www.crabtreebooks.com   1-800-387-7650

Printed in Canada/082015/BF20150630

Published in Canada
Crabtree Publishing
616 Welland Ave.
St. Catharines, Ontario
L2M 5V6

Published in the United States
Crabtree Publishing
PMB 59051
350 Fifth Avenue, 59th Floor
New York, New York 10118

Published in the United Kingdom
Crabtree Publishing
Maritime House
Basin Road North, Hove
BN41 1WR

Published in Australia
Crabtree Publishing
3 Charles Street
Coburg North
VIC, 3058

Contents

What Is Energy?

Waking up, jumping out of bed, going downstairs, and hopping on a stool at the breakfast counter. It all takes energy. So does riding in a car, taking the bus to school, and using your laptop or playing computer games after school. Energy is the ability to do work, and energy comes in many different forms.

A pencil has the **potential energy** to fall to the ground off your desk. Potential energy is stored energy. **Kinetic energy** is energy in motion. When that pencil is falling, it is due to kinetic energy. Energy cannot be created or destroyed. As we see with the pencil, energy can be transformed, or changed, from one type to another.

Mechanical energy uses physical parts you can see, such as the motor in a car, to make things move. **Chemical energy** comes about when one chemical reacts with another. Think about the volcano school project in which baking soda and vinegar mix to make the lava erupt. That is pure chemical energy!

Physical activities such as swimming require energy.

World Energy Consumption

A graph titled "World Energy Consumption" with the y-axis labeled "Exajoules per year" ranging from 0 to 600 (in increments of 100), and the x-axis labeled "Year" ranging from 1820 to 2000 (in increments of 20). The legend shows: nuclear, hydroelectric, natural gas, oil, coal, biofuels.

This graph shows how much of each energy resource we have used over the decades.

To Renew or Not to Renew?

Our energy sources come from **renewable** or **nonrenewable** resources. The Sun is the largest source of energy on Earth. It is a renewable resource that can provide solar power. Solar energy is also responsible for creating wind. Wind energy is growing as a renewable resource. Geothermal energy comes from heat within Earth and hydropower comes from moving water. Biomass power comes from burning plant or organic material. Nonrenewable resources are used up when they serve as fuels. **Fossil fuels** such as oil, natural gas, and coal are nonrenewable. Another type of nonrenewable resource is nuclear energy. Harnessing the power of **atoms** produces nuclear energy. All of these energy sources—both renewable and nonrenewable—can be used to create power such as electricity.

FAST FORWARD

Imagine if you woke up and there was no electricity to make your breakfast, no fuel to heat your home, and no power for your computer. Unfortunately, this is a reality for millions of people around the world. In North America, people are fortunate to have all the energy they need to live. However, unless everyone begins to use energy in a more **sustainable** way, there may be a serious energy shortage in the future. How do you think you would cope if there were less energy to use? Explain what your world might look like.

Energy Consumption

Around the world, fossil fuels are the most commonly used energy resource. Burning coal generates 40 percent of the world's electricity. The United States has less than 5 percent of the world's population, but it uses close to 25 percent of the world's energy.

Fossil fuels are used for most of the nation's electricity production. The United States produces enough energy to meet almost 90 percent of its demand. The remainder of the country's energy needs is met by **importing** oil. The country uses more than 19 million barrels of oil every day. Nuclear power generates about 9 percent, and renewable energy sources provide around 11 percent of the energy needed. Renewable energy production and use in the United States reached record highs in the country in 2014.

This nuclear power plant, along the Rhône River in France, is just one of France's 58 nuclear power plants.

Some States Have It, Some Do Not

Wyoming, Alaska, Louisiana, North Dakota, Iowa, and Texas were the highest energy-consuming states per person in 2012. All of these states—except Louisiana—have very cold winters, which means extra heating fuel is needed during the winter. Some of them also have smaller populations spread out across each state. Transportation is responsible for much of their energy resource use.

The District of Columbia, New York, Rhode Island, California, and Hawaii had the lowest energy use. Warm winters help California and Hawaii limit energy use, but residents of Washington, DC, and New York benefit from living in close quarters with their neighbors. Heat leaving one home is soaked up by the neighbor's home, and so on down the line. A lot of public transportation and short commutes also helped reduce energy consumption in these particular states.

Rush hour slows down traffic and increases the amount of gases vehicles produce.

FAST FORWARD

The world's energy consumption rose 2.3 percent from 2012 to 2013. The world's population is projected to rise from 7.2 billion to 9.6 billion by 2050. There will come a point when coal, oil, and natural gas are no longer available in enough quantities to meet demand. How important do you think renewable energy sources will be in 2050?

How Big Is Our Footprint?

In 1992, scientists Mathis Wackernagel and William Rees developed something called the **ecological footprint.** The ecological footprint is a method for calculating how much land or water a group of humans needs to produce all the resources they use to live. Everyone uses resources, but some people use a lot more than others.

The biggest factor in the growth of the ecological footprint is the **carbon footprint**. The carbon footprint is approximately half of the total ecological footprint. Carbon dioxide is a **greenhouse gas**. About 75 percent of carbon dioxide emissions (gases released) come from burning fossil fuels. The carbon footprint is usually shown in equivalent tons of carbon dioxide and it is figured out over a given period of time, such as one year.

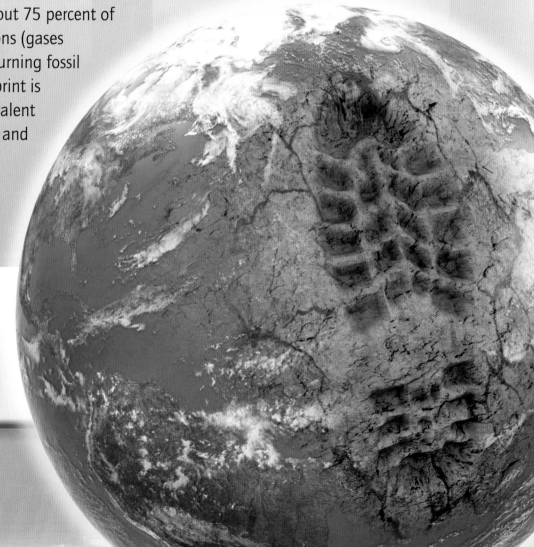

The ecological footprint has more than doubled since 1961. We now need more resources than our planet can produce.

Painting the Carbon Picture

For every one gallon (3.8 liters) of gasoline burned, 19 pounds (8.6 kg) of carbon dioxide is released into the **atmosphere**. Using a computer for just under three days adds 2.2 pounds (1 kg) of carbon dioxide, so does the making of five plastic bags. Global carbon dioxide emissions were close to 44 billion tons (40 billion metric tons) in 2014. That was a 2.5 percent increase over 2013.

India's greenhouse gas emissions are rising steadily. Still, the country's total emissions make up just 6.5 percent of the global total. Emissions of the countries belonging to the European Union (EU) dropped slightly. Total emissions for the EU equal 10 percent of the global figure. China's emissions are increasing. The country now produces 28 percent of global emissions—more than the United States and Europe combined.

The United States has one of the biggest carbon footprints **per capita**. Each person there has a footprint of 18 tons (16 metric tons) per year.

REWIND

The **Industrial Revolution** began in Britain in the mid-1700s. During that time, there was a shift to powered machinery. Factories were built and materials were produced in large quantities. Workers came to live near the factories, and cities grew. Roadways were improved and steam engines began pulling trains. How big do you think the carbon footprint might have been before the Industrial Revolution? Why was that?

Energy and the Environment

Our planet is warming up. Earth's average temperature has increased by over 1.4°Fahrenheit (0.8°C) from 1880 to 2012. It is now warming at a rate of more than 0.2°F (0.1°C) every 10 years. There have been naturally occurring periods of warming and cooling on our planet, but never before have the changes been this dramatic. This rapid change is thought to be a result of greenhouse gases.

Small changes in the average temperature on Earth can have a large impact on the planet's climate and weather. We are already seeing the effects. Around the world, floods, droughts, and heat waves are making the headlines. Our oceans are warming. Glaciers and icecaps are melting at a rapid rate. Sea levels are rising.

The island nation of Maldives has an average elevation of 5 feet (1.5 m) above sea level. It is our planet's lowest country—and the one most in danger from rising sea levels.

Greenhouse Gas Gone Bad

Greenhouse gases, such as carbon dioxide, methane, nitrous oxide, and others, are a natural phenomenon in Earth's atmosphere. These gases trap heat from the Sun and warm our planet. Without them, life would not exist on Earth. The problem comes when these gases are out of balance. Human activity is producing more greenhouse gases than the system can handle.

Rain forests absorb approximately 20 percent of the carbon released by the burning of fossil fuels.

The amount of carbon dioxide in the atmosphere has increased by 42 percent from before the mid 1700s to 2013. Energy use is responsible for two thirds of greenhouse gas emissions because more than 80 percent of global energy consumption is based on fossil fuels. In May 2013, carbon dioxide levels exceeded 400 parts per million for the first time in several hundred thousand years.

FAST FORWARD

Global **climate change** is happening. There is evidence that high-elevation places are warming faster than lower elevations. This affects the rate of **glacial melt**, as well as plant and animal life. Water from high mountains is the main source of water for many people at lower elevations. How do you think you might be affected if these water sources start to dry up?

Use Better Energy

Around the world, the demand for energy is increasing. We need energy to cook our food, light our homes, and drive our cars. In the United States, people started to use more oil than could be produced by the early 1970s. As a result, the country need to bring in more and more imported oil.

In 1973, members of the Organization of Petroleum Exporting Countries (OPEC) placed an oil **embargo** on the United States after the country began supporting Israel in a war with Egypt and Syria. The ban on imports led to fuel shortages, rationing, and soaring prices. As the embargo continued, the American automotive industry began struggling to compete with Japanese manufacturers, which produced more fuel-efficient cars.

Around the same time, the environmental movement was taking hold and started to affect government policies. The United States passed new laws attempting to reduce dependence on fossil fuels and find alternative sources of power. Renewable energy sources were explored. However, oil prices dropped by the mid-1980s and the need for change stalled.

Biomass such as wood is burned as a fuel in many countries in Africa.

Renewable resources are a good idea for meeting the world's energy needs.

Why We Need It

It is estimated that global demand for fuels will go up by 36 percent by the end of 2030. The major reason for this crisis is because our current pattern of energy use is not sustainable. About 1.1 billion people around the world do not have electricity. This is mostly because of the cost and because electricity is not available in places that are hard to reach.

Accessible Alternatives

Affordable and sustainable forms of energy supply must be found that can provide the basic needs for everyone, regardless of income and whether they live in urban places such as towns and cities or on rural properties. In the United States, around 1.3 pounds (0.6 kg) of carbon dioxide is emitted for every **kilowatt-hour** of electricity generated. Once in place, alternative energy sources do not **pollute** the environment or release greenhouse gases.

The Energy Future: You Choose

Alternative resources are sustainable and clean, meaning they do not give off carbon dioxide. But they are not free. Alternative energy production can cost upward of three times as much as some nonrenewable energy production. Those in favor of alternative resources say that their benefits outweigh their costs. What do you think? Find examples in this book to support your answers.

Use Less Energy

Energy **conservation** means using energy less wastefully and more efficiently. Conservation of energy is important because a unit of energy saved is as good as a unit generated. It is far cheaper to save energy by not using it than it is to produce it. Everyone can help by changing their habits.

Less Is More

Walk around your house at night and count the little lights shining on your electronic devices and **appliances**. Although these appliances are not actually working, they are still using energy. Televisions, DVD players, stereos, and computers still use 10 to 60 percent of power, even when on stand-by. Up to 24 coal-fired power stations could be closed if users in industrialized countries unplugged chargers and switched off home appliances instead of putting them on stand-by.

The amount of energy used to light a house can be reduced by installing energy-efficient light bulbs. Compact fluorescent bulbs use one quarter of the electricity of a traditional light bulb. They also last up to eight times longer. Do not forget when you leave a room to turn off the lights!

This Mitsubishi electric car has no gas tank or exhaust pipe. It does not emit any greenhouse gases.

Use Power Wisely

People can save electricity by turning off televisions, computers, and other electronic devices when they are not in use. Laptop computers use five times less electricity than desktop computers, so switching to a laptop will save power. Enabling the power management function on a computer will save electricity, too.

We can also conserve energy by using energy-efficient machines and vehicles. An average car emits approximately three times its weight in carbon dioxide per year. Walk or bike to your friend's house instead of going by car. Put on another layer of clothes instead of turning up the thermostat in winter. Simple changes can have a big effect.

Unplug chargers for smartphones and other mobile devices when you are not using them.

FAST FORWARD

Think about all the ways that you can save electricity. Do you think it is possible to make significant changes in our energy usage in the next 15 years? Will it be enough to reduce greenhouse gas emissions? Explain your thinking.

Think Global, Act Local

We know that around the world, the climate is changing. We also know it is changing faster than ever before because of too many greenhouse gases in the atmosphere and that people's use of energy is tied to the production of these greenhouse gases. We need to look at what changes can be made to do our part in addressing the problem. That is what it means to "think global, act local."

The phrase "think global, act local" took center stage as an environmental slogan in the early 1970s. Today, it is often tied to climate change. Our lives are connected to the climate. A warming climate will bring changes that can affect water supplies, agriculture, power and transportation systems, the natural environment, and even our own health and safety. There is an obvious question: "What can we do about it?"

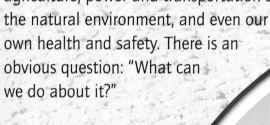

The date on this marker for a glacier in Jasper National Park is clear evidence of a warming climate.

The glacier was here in
Le glacier était ici en

1908

All for One and One for All

As individuals, we cannot make global climate change disappear. Carbon dioxide can stay in the atmosphere for nearly a century, so Earth will continue to warm in the coming decades. The warmer it gets, the greater the risk for more severe changes to the climate and Earth's system. The problem is just too large for one person to make a difference.

However, if we look closely at climate change, we see how energy use is at the root of the problem. People can act as individuals to make a difference on a local level in the short term. They can take action at home, on the road, and in schools to help reduce greenhouse gas emissions.

In addition to being good for the environment, **organic** food is good for you because it contains no harmful chemicals.

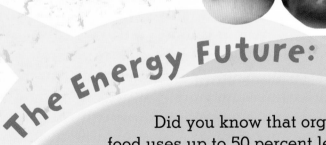

The Energy Future: You Choose

Did you know that organic food uses up to 50 percent less energy during production than nonorganic food? If that organic vegetable is grown locally, then energy is also saved in transportation. On the other hand, it does take more human labor to farm organically. This means an increased cost. Do you think organic, locally grown food saves enough energy to make it worth the extra effort and cost to produce it? Would you pay more to get it?

Sustainable Living

Sustainable living is being able to meet the needs of the present without affecting the ability of future **generations** to meet their own needs. It means leaving enough resources on Earth for our children and their children to survive. It is a lifestyle that reduces the use of Earth's natural resources on personal, community, and national levels.

Often, sustainable living comes down to reducing the carbon footprint. Everyone can do this by reducing their energy consumption. People are looking seriously at cleaner, more reliable sources of electricity. Governments are searching for low-carbon development options. Renewable resources, such as wind and solar power, are becoming more affordable.

People are starting to campaign for change.

Purchasing Power

Clean energy is here. Today, these energy sources are small, but they are rapidly expanding. Since 2008, the price of solar panels has fallen by 75 percent. If solar panels were added to 80 percent of **commercial** buildings in the United States, it would be the same as turning off 33 coal-fired power plants for one year. Since 2008, the cost of electric vehicle batteries has dropped by 50 percent. Comparing purchases in the first six months of 2011 with the first six months of 2013, people in the United States bought six times as many electric cars.

The cost of super-efficient light-emitting diode (LED) lights has fallen more than 85 percent. As a result, sales have skyrocketed. In 2009, there were fewer than 400,000 LED lights installed in the United States. Today, that number is almost 20 million. If every home in the United States replaced just five of its most-used light bulbs with more efficient bulbs, it would have the same effect as taking 10 million cars from the road.

Small homes use less energy, and apartments with five or more solar units in the building are the most energy-efficient.

FAST FORWARD

Imagine yourself living in 2030. Clean energy will dominate your world. Sustainable living will not be just a catch phrase. It will be how you live your life on a daily basis. Describe your future home and community with regards to how you will use energy on a daily basis.

The Energy Island

Small, low-elevation islands are facing the effects of climate change head on. Islands are at risk of serious damage from rising sea levels and more intense and frequent storms. Some islands are becoming models for sustainable living and lowering their carbon footprint by depending on 100 percent clean, renewable energy.

On the Mark

The Danish island of Samsø was the first island in the world to become completely powered by renewable energy. A model renewable energy community, the island has installed 11 land-based and 10 **offshore** wind turbines to meet the electricity needs of the approximately 4,000 residents. Sustainable energy sources provide 70 percent of the island's heating.

The offshore turbines produce so much energy that they make up for the greenhouse gases produced by oil-fired boilers and gas- and diesel-powered vehicles. This makes the island carbon dioxide neutral. The island's goal is to become fossil-fuel free by 2030. Samsø has been called the "Energy Island."

Winds on the Baltic Sea are used to generate Samsø's electricity.

Small but Determined Changes

Tokelau is a series of three small islands in the South Pacific. The tallest point on all of the islands is less than 17 feet (5.2 m) above sea level. Climate change and rising sea levels are a huge problem for the people who live there. In 2012, the nation switched from diesel-powered generators burning 211 gallons (800 l) of fuel a day to 100 percent renewable energy. Solar panels and storage batteries provide more electricity than island residents can use.

The island of El Hierro is at the western edge of Spain's Canary Islands. With more than 10,000 inhabitants, the island produced 18,800 tons (17,055 metric tons) of carbon dioxide each year. That is, until it switched to renewable energy sources. Now, wind turbines, solar panels, and hydroelectricity provide all its energy.

Coal, oil, and gas are slowly being replaced by sustainable energy sources.

REWIND

The tiny Isle of Eigg off the west coast of Scotland is almost completely energy self-sufficient. In 1997, the community bought the island and decided renewable energy could transform the energy system. They were right. Today, Eigg has its own independent energy grid with wind, solar, and hydropower sites. Why do you think it might be easier for a small island to become sustainable than for a large country?

Building a Green Community

Half of today's global population lives in cities. By 2030, the world's cities are expected to add 1.5 billion people. There will be up to an additional 1 billion cars. The problem is that cities are responsible for more than 70 percent of the global carbon dioxide emissions related to energy use. The solution is to tackle climate change by changing the cities.

The way that cities have been developed in the past increases greenhouse gas emissions. If cities are built with an eye toward efficiency, they can fight climate change. Cities need to become sustainable and more **accessible**, or easy to get around. Green communities should be kept in mind when planning our future cities.

Green Is Gold

Civano in Tucson, Arizona, is a green community. Solar power, sustainable building materials, and water conservation technologies are key elements in the community. The community is designed to put homes, shopping areas, schools, parks, and workplaces within walking distance of each other as often as possible. This helps **conserve**, or save, resources and minimize waste.

Midtown Manhattan, which includes Times Square, uses more energy thz an the whole country of Kenya.

The Prescott Passive House in Kansas City, Kansas, uses many smart energy-efficient features to use minimal energy.

Toronto in Canada was the first city in North America to require green roofs on new industrial buildings. Green roofs are partly covered with living plants such as grasses. They provide extra insulation, absorb rainwater, and help lower air temperatures in urban areas.

Recipe for Success

Green communities have buildings that are energy efficient with most or all of the community's energy coming from renewable resources. Waste reduction and reusing are components of everyday life in these communities. Having nearby local services reduces the need to travel and encourages cycling or walking, rather than driving.

FAST FORWARD

Passive houses are super-insulated, airtight buildings. They have energy recovery ventilation to remove stale, polluted air and replace it with fresh, outdoor air while still conserving energy. Their windows prevent heat transfer in and out of the home. The idea of passive homes began in the United States and Canada, but has really taken off in Europe. Do you think passive homes are something builders should promote more in the future? Explain why or why not.

Greening Your School

Many schools are finding ways to use energy as efficiently as possible. Green schools set an example for their students and communities. They also save money by reducing energy demand and conserving natural resources.

Green schools are either built without **toxic**, or poisonous, materials or have worked to remove hazardous materials in places where children learn and play. Green schools manage the use of daylight to reduce the need for artificial lights in classrooms. They buy sustainable products and practice green, environmentally friendly cleaning techniques. They encourage **recycling** and promote **habitat** protection. They also help students become **environmentally literate**. That means someone has the ability to understand the health of natural systems and to take action to maintain, restore, or improve the health of those systems.

This specially designed bamboo and tile school in Bali, Indonesia, was a 2012 winner of the "Greenest School on Earth" award. The school uses renewable resources, grows much of the food it consumes, and is involved in ground-breaking environmental projects.

There are some schools that are dated and in need of repair to bring them up to green standards, but others are built to be green. The Lady Bird Johnson Middle School in Irving, Texas, was the first green school in the state. Solar, wind, and geothermal energy are used to generate electricity. **Passive solar energy** lights the inside during the day. An interactive museum and solar panel observation deck provide learning opportunities for students of the school.

Put It to Work

There are many things that students can do to help "green" their schools. Starting an eco-group to brainstorm ways of reducing the school's carbon footprint encourages green thinking. Students can look at ways to rearrange classrooms to increase energy efficiency. For example, putting reading tables near windows is an easy fix. Turning off lights, unplugging appliances when they are not in use, using energy-saving light bulbs, shutting off computers, and using smart power strips are just some of the ways schools can be greener without needing major alterations.

Reduce, reuse, and recycle is the sustainable living motto.

FAST FORWARD

Environmental literacy is being able to understand environmental systems and to make an effort to maintain or improve the health of those systems. Energy use affects the environment. What would you recommend be done in your school to promote environmental literacy in the future? What part could you play in getting this movement started?

Going Green at Home

The demand for energy is increasing every year. We are continuously harnessing the energy resources available on our planet to meet these energy demands. One day, these resources might be used up and there will be nothing left to meet our energy needs. We must start conserving energy now.

There are simple things people can start doing at home. Riding a bike instead of traveling by car is much better for the environment. Taking the bus is also better because **mass transportation** uses less energy than personal vehicles.

After doing laundry, it will save electricity if clothes are dried on a rack or outdoors instead of in a dryer. By adjusting the temperature on the hot water tank to 140°F (60°C) or lower, up to 10 percent in energy costs can be saved. When houses need to be repainted, bright colors are better. Bright colors on walls and ceilings reflect more light, reducing the need for artificial lighting throughout the day. They also help keep the house cooler, which means less need for air conditioning.

We all have a hand in using energy wisely.

Star Choices

It saves electricity when families eat dinner together because the food does not need to be heated every time someone is ready to eat—the food will taste better fresh, anyway! When kitchen appliances need to be replaced, their replacements' energy rating should be checked. Energy Star appliances are rated high for energy efficiency. They use 10 to 15 percent less energy than regular appliances.

Other home improvements that save energy include digital thermostats that can be programmed and energy-efficient windows and doors. People may not want a lawn on their roofs, but adding a few solar panels or maybe a residential wind turbine can all make a difference.

Infrared thermal cameras detect heat loss from homes. The red parts of the image are the hottest places, followed by orange and yellow.

FAST FORWARD

In the future, if energy use outpaces energy production, we may not have enough electricity to run our electronics or warm our homes. We many not have the fuel to power our vehicles. How do you think this will affect society as a whole? Explain your thinking.

Power Up!

We all need energy to live, but how we use power at home, school, and work says a lot about our willingness to help our planet. Saving energy is not always the easiest path to follow. Sometimes, it means giving up things we think we need.

What Can You Do?

We do not always know what we can do until we investigate our energy use. Do you know how well your classroom does in the energy game? Are there any alternative sources of energy used to power your school? Where could your classroom improve when it comes to energy conservation? These are all questions that can be answered when you participate in a classroom **energy audit**. An energy audit is a review of all of the energy use in a particular area.

Explore the energy alternatives—you never know what you might discover!

Activity

In this test, you will examine your classroom—or the whole school if everyone will participate—for its basic energy use, as well as areas where energy might be conserved.

You Will Need:

- A pencil
- Paper

	used for	number in the classroom	left on overnight
desktop computers			
laptops			
tablets			
printers			
DVD/VCR players			
LCD projectors			
stereo			
television			
smart board			
sound system			
phone chargers			

Instructions

1. List all of the electronic devices you see in the classroom. Make a note of the number of desktop computers, laptops, tablets, printers, DVD/VCR players, LCD projectors, as well as devices such as a stereo, television, smart board, sound system, phone chargers, and any other devices powered by electricity.
2. Find out whether each device is left on in active mode overnight, set to sleep or low-power mode, or turned off completely. Plugging appliances into a power strip is like unplugging them if the power strip is turned off at the end of the day. Write down the way each device is used.
3. How many lights are in your classroom?
4. What types of light bulbs are used (fluorescent tubes, incandescent bulbs, or compact fluorescent bulbs)?
5. How much energy does each bulb use?
6. For how many hours is each bulb turned on each day?
7. Does the school have solar panels or wind turbines?

Pass or Fail?

Energy audits allow us to look at our current energy usage. The audit can be used as the basis for action to save energy. Does it feel as though your classroom is energy-efficient? What changes would you suggest for improving your classroom energy consumption?

Glossary

Please note: Some bold-faced words are defined where they appear in the text

appliances Instruments or devices designed for household use and operated by electricity

atmosphere The layers of gases that surround Earth

atoms The smallest possible parts of an element

climate change Changes to the usual weather patterns in an area or the entire Earth

commercial Business or for profit

conservation Slowing down or stopping the use of something so it will still be around in the future

embargo An official ban on trade with a particular country

energy audit A measure of how much energy is used and finding out where it is wasted

fossil fuels Energy sources made from the remains of plants and animals that died millions of years ago and were buried

generations Groups of people who are born and live at around the same time

glacial melt The runoff water that comes from a melting glacier

greenhouse gas A gas in the atmosphere that contributes to the greenhouse effect

habitat The place where a plant or animal usually lives

importing Bringing in goods or services from another country

Industrial Revolution A rapid change in which countries become more focused on using machines to make goods

kilowatt-hour Getting 1 watt of power for one hour

mass transportation Shared public transportation that can carry many people at once

nonrenewable Something that does not renew itself once it is used up

offshore In the ocean, some distance from the land

organic Describes foods produced without artificial chemicals or a material that was formerly living and contains carbon

passive solar energy Taking advantage of natural energy characteristics in materials and air created by exposure to the Sun

per capita Per person

pollute To release into the environment a substance that is harmful or poisonous to plants, animals, or people

recycling Converting waste into reusable materials

renewable Something that renews itself
  once it is used

sustainable Describing a way of living
  that conserves and efficiently uses
  natural resources

Learning More

Find out more about energy and living in a sustainable way.

Books

Drummond, Allan. *Energy Island: How One Community Harnessed the Wind and Changed Their World*. Square Fish, 2015.

Johnson, John Jr. *Living Green* (Sally Ride Science). Flash Point, 2010.

Lanz, Helen. *Shopping Choices* (Go Green). Sea-to-Sea, 2012.

Senker, Cath. *A Teen guide to Being Eco in Your Community* (Eco Guides). Heinemann-Raintree, 2013.

Websites

Visit the website below to learn about a career as a home energy auditor:
http://climatekids.nasa.gov/career-auditor

A student's guide to global climate change:
http://epa.gov/climatechange/kids/index.html

Calculate your personal ecological footprint and see how to change it at:
www.footprintnetwork.org

Index